INTRODUCTION

This is the play that's based on the books that are based on the idea that history is full of people doing horrible things to one another. History is the story of man's inhumanity to man ... not to mention woman, child, animal and planet.

Not satisfied with torturing one another for a million years, human beings came up with a new and horrible way of making children suffer: the history lesson! "Learn this! You'll be tested on that! People don't matter, dates matter! Humanity doesn't matter, *facts* matter! I'm going to suck all the life-blood out of those facts and feed your minds on the driest dust that is left."

Now the truth fights back. It won't be sucked dry any longer. In these books the gore and guts gush back in, the foul facts come to the forefront and the cruel crimes are no longer concealed from the kids. Teachers are trembling in terror as the tables are turned.

Knowledge is power; horrible history is the most powerful knowledge of all.

This play looks at the maddest millennium at its end. It explores the question: why do people behave the way they do? And you may end up asking: why do I behave the way I do? Along the way you may even ask: how have we humans survived this long?

STAGING

The setting is Britain – any time in the last 1000 years. It is also a 1999 Music and Drama Studio where blackout, stage-lighting, sound and music are all available against a backdrop/cyclorama that can change colour as characters slip from the present into a variety of ages and scenes. There is a roller blackboard, a costume hamper, a tape player, a lighting console and an electronic keyboard. There is a prop box, which contains an axe, a microphone, a dummy's head, and a variety of torture instruments – see *Bloody Scotland* page 110 for reference. At the back of the stage is a large, back-less book cupboard. There are also movable stage-blocks that double as seats and sets, and a chair centre stage with clamps on the arms.

In the 1999 Drama Room there are seven students. They wear no school uniform as such but each wears a combination of two of the play's basic colours: blood red, parchment cream, monk brown, Robin Hood green and bat black. The teacher is the only one to wear all black. As the pupils assume the role of a character from the past they add a simple piece of costume in one of the basic colours.

To Cecily, John, Kathryn, Patricia and Peter,
the original members of Theatr Powys.
And in special memory of Dennis Hunt, our
"Godfather", who died July 1998. Thanks.

Scholastic Children's Books,
Commonwealth House, 1–19 New Oxford Street,
London WC1A 1NU, UK

A division of Scholastic Ltd
London ~ New York ~ Toronto ~ Sydney ~ Auckland
Mexico City ~ New Delhi ~ Hong Kong

Published in the UK by Scholastic Ltd, 1999

Text copyright © Terry Deary, 1999
Cover illustration copyright © Martin Brown, 1999

ISBN 0 439 01379 8

All rights reserved
Typeset by TW Typesetting, Midsomer Norton, Somerset
Printed by Cox & Wyman Ltd, Reading, Berks

2 4 6 8 10 9 7 5 3 1

STAGING FOR SCHOOLS

There are eight characters ... but they play a couple of dozen parts between them. If your theatre company has a lot of actors wanting parts then you can cast it differently: give the seven students and their teacher their parts, but when they switch to historical characters you can bring in new actors to play them, and adapt the text slightly.

HORRIBLE HISTORIES

The facts and anecdotes in *The Mad Millennium* play are taken from the following *Horrible Histories* books published by Scholastic Children's Books, written by Terry Deary and illustrated by Martin Brown: *The Rotten Romans*, *The Vicious Vikings*, *Cruel Kings and Mean Queens* (illustrated by Kate Sheppard), *The Measly Middle Ages*, *Wicked Words* (illustrated by Philip Reeve), *Even More Terrible Tudors*, *The Slimy Stuarts*, *The Gorgeous Georgians*, *The Vile Victorians*, *The Frightful First World War*. Additional material comes from *True War Stories* in Scholastic's Point Non-Fiction series, also by Terry Deary.

CHARACTERS

The students have distinctive characteristics in 1999 and, when they slip into their historical roles, some of these characteristics travel with them. So Henry Bull in 1999, for example, can easily adopt the role of Bully Henry VIII in 1536. Similarly, the tensions between the students are mirrored in the scenes from the past.

JAMES ABBOTT	Pompous and pedantic, with a disdain for his fellow pupils and a desire to be treated as an equal of the teacher.
HENRY BULL	Abrasive and confident on the surface, but with an unpleasant slyness and capacity for hypocrisy.
WILL CHESTER	The class clown, always trying to turn situations into a joke; needs attention. He is also the principal musician with keyboard skills.
EDWARD DOE	Painfully shy and lacking in confidence, mainly because of his struggle with reading.
ELIZABETH REGENT	Angry and passionate about justice and equality though sometimes insensitive to those in need of her support.

MARY STREET	Precocious and energetic. Naturally inquisitive and bright but reluctant to be seen as an academic.
CATHERINE TRAIN	A born "follower", hanging on the coat tails of Mary or whoever holds the upper hand.
MASTER MINDE	History teacher. Sinister and shadowy figure who for most of the play is only a presence through a voice on a recorder.
MISS GAME	Drama teacher. Enthusiastic and capable, but with a darker side that the pupils fail to see.

The Mad Millennium was first performed at the
Sherman Theatre, Cardiff on 4 June 1999.

Directed by Phil Clark
Designed by Sean Crowley
Lighting designed by Ceri James

At the time of printing, this script was still in rehearsal
and therefore some changes to the text will not have
been incorporated in this edition of the play.

ACT ONE

SCENE ONE

Pupils enter classroom talking over the top of one another about the exams and the last lesson. "HISTORY" is chalked on the roller blackboard with instructions disappearing under the board.

MARY: I've lost my timetable! What lesson's next?

JAMES: Actually, Mary, it's History.

HENRY: (*mocking*) Actually that's jolly bad news, James, old chap.

CATHERINE: Yeah! I hated it last year.

ELIZABETH: Oh, Catherine! It was only bad last year because Miss Fitt was a hopeless teacher.

WILL: Yeah, fatty Fitt was a *mis*-fit all right.

JAMES: We have a Mr Minde this year, it says on my timetable. Who's he?

MARY: New teacher.

JAMES: But we're in the Performing Arts Studio?

MARY: Probably the only room free at this time.

WILL: Hey! If Mr Minde's a schoolmaster we can call him Master Minde! Mastermind – geddit?

HENRY: (*sourly*) History will *still* be horrible.

WILL: Horrible History? That's a good name, Henry.

(He goes to the keyboard in the corner and picks out a simple sequence of notes, then begins to sing.)

Ho-rib-bull Hiss-tor-ree, Ho-rib-bull Hiss-tor-ree.

(The other children begin to pick up the tune.)

MARY: *Ho-rib-bull Hiss-tor-ree, why we have to learn it's a miss-tor-ree!*

ALL: *Ho-rib-bull Hiss-tor-ree, why we have to learn it's a miss-tor-ree!*

HENRY: *That Julius Caesar was such an odd geezer,*
He had a big nose and he called it his sneezer!

ALL: *Ho-rib-bull Hiss-tor-ree, why we have to learn it's a miss-tor-ree!*

MARY: *That Eric the Red murdered kids in their bed,*
But old age caught up with him, now he is dead!

ALL: *(Chorus)*

ELIZABETH: *King Alfred the Great, burned the cakes*

10

	on a plate,
	So he never got fat like king Henry the Eight!
ALL:	(*Chorus*)
CATHERINE:	*Guy Fawkes had a plot to turn parliament hot,*
	With a bomb underneath old King James's fat bot!
ALL:	(*Chorus*)
JAMES:	Catherine … please! (*Looks at audience, horrified*) You can't say that. There are some of the new first–years in the corridor. (*He names some pupils from the audience.*)
CATHERINE:	Ah! Sorry, James, Sorry, James! Sorry, sorry, sorry!
HENRY:	So you give us a verse, clever-features.
JAMES:	*In wars against France, fought with sword and with lance,*
	The English won glory…
WILL:	*…but then lost their pants!*
ELIZABETH:	Will, you'll never get anywhere if you don't take your lessons seriously.
WILL:	What? Like History?
	(*Sings chorus. Turns to* EDWARD *who is looking at blackboard.*)
WILL:	Your verse, Edward!

EDWARD: (*panicked*) I – I – I can't. I'm no good at poetry.

HENRY: You're no good at *anything* Edward Doe. Doe by name, dope by nature. How are you going to do in the exams? Eh?

CATHERINE: Yeah, Edward. How *are* you going to do?

HENRY: Let's see, shall we?

(HENRY *pushes* EDWARD *into chair and rolls board to reveal map of Europe.*)

HENRY: The Romans conquered Italy, they conquered Europe then they conquered southern England. Then they stopped. Why?

EDWARD: They ran out of conkers?

(*The others laugh and begin to circle* EDWARD.)

HENRY: They stopped at Hadrian's Wall. Where's Hadrian's Wall?

EDWARD: At the bottom of Hadrian's garden?

HENRY: They divided Gaul into three parts. How?

EDWARD: Did they use a pair of Caesars?

HENRY: And when Caesar's friend Brutus stabbed him, what famous words did Caesar say?

EDWARD: Ouch?

HENRY: I said *words*!

EDWARD: Ouch! Ouch! Ouch! (HENRY *grabs his ear and twists*) Ouch! Ouch! Ouch!

(MISS GAME *enters and stands at door.*)

MISS GAME: What are you doing to that boy?

HENRY: Teaching him some history, Miss … er, Miss…

MISS GAME: I'm Miss Game. Here on supply. So, you're a history expert are you?

HENRY: I would be. I just can't be bothered to learn the boring dates.

MISS GAME: Or to read the blackboard, it seems.

HENRY: You what?

MISS GAME: Mr Minde has been delayed in Egypt.

WILL: What's he doing in Egypt?

MISS GAME: He's an archaeologist. He's unwrapping mummies buried in the Valley of the Kings.

MARY: Why's he unwrapping them?

WILL: 'Cos they're too dead to unwrap themselves, stupid.

MISS GAME: He'll be back by the end of the day but he sent a tape of instructions for this class. I'm just a cover teacher till he arrives. But I wrote his instructions on the board.

(JAMES *rolls board to reveal message under the "HISTORY" title, which he reads.*)

JAMES: "History class. Your instructions are on the tape. Press PLAY."

ELIZABETH: Sorry, Miss, we didn't see it.

CATHERINE: We didn't see it, Miss.

MARY: Just play it and see what the wrinklie wants.

(*She presses button. The voice is deep and menacing and loud.*)

MINDE: This class comes to me with a reputation for being idle, insolent and argumentative. (*They react*) You will all change.

WILL: I changed my socks just last month!

MINDE: When I return I will test you all on the history of Britain over the last millennium. Anyone who fails the test will be punished like no pupil has ever been punished. You may think you have suffered in the past. But you have yet to suffer the horror of history.

CATHERINE: He scares me!

HENRY: I'm not afraid of some stupid teacher.

CATHERINE: No. Sorry, that's what I meant to say. He *doesn't* scare me!

MINDE: All the books you need are in the

cupboard. Start with the Norman
Conquest in 1066. Get the books out
and get started – or else.

JAMES: He can't threaten us like that!

MINDE: You have been warned. I have powers
that no other teacher ever had.

JAMES: I'll get his rotten books and burn them.

(*He marches to the cupboard, throws open
the door and screams in terror as the brilliant
image of a monstrous mummy with glowing
eyes lurks there. He screams, which sets
off* CATHERINE. *He slams the door shut.*)

HENRY: (*sitting in chair, centre stage*) He can't
make *me* do the work!

(*A crackling flash of light strikes him and
gives him an electric shock. He is
paralysed with fear.*)

ELIZABETH: I'm not standing for this!

(*She marches to door. She grasps the
handle which glows red and sizzles. She
shrinks back to her desk.*)

ELIZABETH: It's hot!

MINDE: You don't leave this room unless you

	pass the test. Some of you may never leave.
EDWARD:	Perhaps we'd better do what he tells us.
CATHERINE:	You're right Edward. (*She marches up to tape recorder and shouts into speaker*) Sorry, Sir. We was only joking.

(*There is an echoing laugh from the machine that makes her jump back.*)

MARY:	(*approaching teacher*) Will you help us, Miss Game?
MISS GAME:	I'm a drama teacher, not a historian.
MARY:	But with the books, Miss.
JAMES:	It's not fair! I just tried to get the books and that … thing in the cupboard wouldn't let me.
EDWARD:	It wouldn't let you *burn* them. Maybe it would let you take them out to study them.
MARY:	That's daft, Dope. The cupboard can't *know* why you want them.
ELIZABETH:	Give him a chance. Let *him* go to the cupboard.
HENRY:	Yeah, let *him* pee himself when that monster leaps out.

(*The class watch as* EDWARD *walks to the cupboard. He opens it. He takes out the books.*)

CATHERINE: I knew it would be all right. Give the books out, Edward.

JAMES: Excuse me, Miss Game, but are you trapped in here too?

(*She goes to the door and the handle glows red.*)

MISS GAME: Looks like it. We're alone.

JAMES: (*pointing at audience*) Except for those kids in the corridor. (*All characters turn and look out towards auditorium*) I wonder if they can see us? Hello? Can you see us? (*To others*) They can! I wonder if they'll be able to help us?

HENRY: Nah! They all look a bit thick to me!

EDWARD: Maybe if we asked them nicely.

HENRY: (*mimics*) Maybe if we ask them *nicely*? Look, if they refuse to help us we just smack them round the head a few times.

EDWARD: But we can't get out to do that!

ELIZABETH: He's right.

CATHERINE: He's right you know.

HENRY: (*menacing*) If those kids let me down then I'll get out there and get them!

EDWARD: If they let you down then you won't be able to get out. They're safe.

17

CATHERINE: He's right, you know!

HENRY: (*to audience*) You'd better help … *or else*!

EDWARD: They might if you said "please".

CATHERINE: Great idea!

HENRY: (*turning on her*) What?

CATHERINE: Er… Stupid idea!

JAMES: Look, we have Miss Game to help with the drama – the books for the facts … plus, of course, I know an awful lot. Let's get started, shall we?

SCENE TWO

The lights dim and the students adopt costumes and props.

JAMES: The Measly Middle Ages really began when William, Duke of Normandy, invaded England. (*He places Norman helmet on* WILL*'s head and hands him a sword.*)

HENRY: But not without a fight from brave Harry the English leader. (*Puts on crown*)

EDWARD: I guess you could blame Edward.

HENRY:⎫ (*as Harold, and William of Normandy*)
WILL: ⎭ You certainly could.

JAMES: Edward the Confessor, a saintly king, was dying.

18

(EDWARD *lies down while* ELIZABETH *and* MARY, *as nuns, tend to him.* CATHERINE, *as Edward's wife, Queen Edith, weeps.* MISS GAME, *as hooded Death with a scythe, stands over him*)

EDWARD: (*as Edward the Confessor*) I am dying!

MARY: (*as nun*) Booey-hooey! Booey-hooey!

ELIZABETH: (*as nun*) Fear not, Queen Edith, your husband is a saint.

CATHERINE: (*as Queen Edith, dramatic and sincere*) And, when the saints go marching in, *he*'s gonna be there in that number.

(WILL *strikes a chord on the organ. The girls leap up and do an outrageous and loud version of "When the Saints Go Marching In". Second time around they urge audience participation. At the last great chord* EDWARD *calls out...*)

EDWARD: (*as Edward the Confessor*) Oi! You lot! Can't a king die in peace?

CATHERINE: (*as Queen Edith, outraged at audience even though she led the singing*) Yeah, you lot! Can't a king die in peace.

HENRY: (*as Harold*) Not until he's named his successor.

CATHERINE: (*as Queen Edith, to* EDWARD) Not until

you've named your successor, you dope.

EDWARD: (*as Edward the Confessor*) Oh, I don't know. My brother-in-law Harold has looked after the country while I have been doing good works. I suppose I should name him.

CATHERINE: (*as Queen Edith, thumbs up to* HENRY) Looks like you got the job, brother!

WILLIAM: (*as William of Normandy*) Just a minute! Two years ago you promised the throne to me, William of Normandy! You even sent Harold over with the message. (*Jabs* HENRY *with forefinger*) And *you* swore on a box of Holy relics to support me.

HENRY: (*as Harold*) Ah! But I had my fingers crossed so it doesn't count! Nyah-nah!

WILLIAM: (*as William of Normandy*) Now who gets your throne, old man?

EDWARD: (*as Edward the Confessor*) Oh, sort it out between you!

JAMES: And then Edward did a silly, but saintly thing.

EDWARD: (*as Edward the Confessor*) I died!

(MISS GAME, *as Death, leads him from his death bed.*)

CATHERINE: (*as Queen Edith*) Booey-hooey!

HENRY: (*as Harold, squaring up to* WILLIAM) No time for tears. Time to defend against the Norman invasions!

CATHERINE: (*as Queen Edith*) Look out, Harry! It's William of Normandy, landed at Hastings!

(*The actors gather into two groups around* WILL *and* HENRY. HENRY *and supporters leap on to a box to claim the higher ground.*)

HENRY: (*as Harold, to* EDWARD *who is by his side as an English soldier*) Stay on the hilltop! He'll never be able to defeat us while we stay on the hilltop!

JAMES: (*as a Norman soldier, narrating as he acts out the manoeuvres*) He was right! We fought uphill all day ... but every time we reached the top ... they pushed us back. We were slipping on the blood of our own dead!

WILL: (*as William of Normandy*) One last attack!

JAMES: (*as a Norman soldier*) We failed again! But this time the English followed us down!

(JAMES *falls to his knees.* EDWARD, *as English soldier, jumps down and stands over him.* WILL *is behind* EDWARD.)

21

HENRY: (*as Harold*) No! You fool!

    (EDWARD *falls and* MISS GAME, *as Death, takes him away.*)

MISS GAME: (*as Death*) Back for you later, Harold!

JAMES: William of Normandy led the massacre and then turned back to the hill.

WILL: (*as William of Normandy*) Archers! Fire!

    (*The girls carry arrows in an arc towards* HENRY *and stab at him as he cowers. He snatches at one and screams and tugs at it. The arrow appears to be in his eye*)

JAMES: (*as a Norman soldier*) With their leader Harold wounded, the English didn't stop us this time.

    (*They act it out while* ELIZABETH *narrates.*)

ELIZABETH: A bishop described what happened next. "The first Norman knight split Harold's chest, driving the point of his sword through the king's shield. The gushing torrent of blood drenched the earth. The second knight struck off his

22

head below the helmet and the third
stabbed the inside of his belly with a
lance. The fourth cut off his leg and
carried it away."

MISS GAME: *(as Death)* I told you I'd be back for
you!

WILL: And that's how William the Conqueror
won the battle of Hastings and changed
British history for ever.

SCENE THREE

*Lights change back to school setting and students take
off their costumes and put away the props.* WILL *stands
at keyboard.*

WILL: *Ho-rib-bull Hiss-tor-ree, why we have
to learn it's a miss-tor-ree!*

ALL: *Ho-rib-bull Hiss-tor-ree, why we have
to learn it's a miss-tor-ree!*

HENRY: *(recites) So poor Harold died, and a
whole nation cried,
Thanks to one lucky shot and a poke in
the eye!*

(He grabs EDWARD *by shirt front
threateningly)*

HENRY: William didn't win the Battle of Hastings. It was Harold's bean-brained soldiers that lost it for him. Why did you charge down the hill?

CATHERINE: Yeah, it was all your fault, Ed!

MISS GAME: (*gently*) It's only a story, Henry. Put Edward down.

CATHERINE: Yeah! Put him down. You don't know where he's been!

MARY: That's all wrong, Miss!

MISS GAME: What, Mary?

MARY: The story! Harold died with an arrow in his eye. Everyone knows that!

ELIZABETH: (*points to book*) But the Bishop was there. The arrow in the eye *wounded* Harold but it didn't kill him!

HENRY: So our history teachers got it wrong, eh? (*Shouts at tape recorder*) Don't know everything do you, musty Minde?

MINDE: (*voice*) I do know that you won't get out of this room unless you know a lot more.

MARY: So what happened next?

JAMES: (*with book*) William took over England. When the English tried to stand up to him he massacred them. (*Reads*) "In York his soldiers massacred every man woman and child they came across. Then they destroyed their homes and their crops. The roads were littered

24

	with corpses and survivors stayed alive by eating them!"
MARY:	Cannibals! That's sick! If I'd met William the Conqueror I'd have … I'd have...
WILL:	Eaten him?
JAMES:	He was no worse than the other kings in the Measly Middle Ages. His son, William the Second, was even crueller!

(WILL *jumps on to stage block and strikes a pose.*)

WILL:	I'm William the Second. I love hunting deer.
CATHERINE:	So hunt me, Will! I'm a dear!
WILL:	(*mimes shooting arrow*) Got you!
CATHERINE:	Oh dear! Oh dear! Oh dear! He shot me in the eye.
WILL:	I say, I say, I say! What do you call a deer with one eye missing?
ALL:	(*wearily*) No-eye deer!
WILL:	And what do you call a dead deer with one eye missing?
ALL:	Still no-eye deer!
MARY:	Somebody should have shot William!
MISS GAME:	Oh but they did. One day William the Second was out hunting in the forest when one of his huntsmen killed him

	with an arrow. He said it was an accident!
MARY:	I bet it was murder! Who got the throne?
MISS GAME:	His brother … Henry!
HENRY:	That's me!
MISS GAME:	And Henry had been hunting in the same forest that day.
WILL:	Murderer!
HENRY:	(*laughing*) Not joking now, are you, Will?
ELIZABETH:	Stop arguing. We have to get through thirty odd kings and queens before the test! How will we do it, Miss?
MISS GAME:	Try simple rhymes to help them stick.
JAMES:	Wonderful idea, Miss, if I may say so. Stephen and Matilda came next. He surrounded her in a castle and she escaped through the snow disguised in a white cloak!
ELIZABETH:	(*sits* MARY *on the central chair which becomes the throne*) Let's see what rhyme we can come up with…

ELIZABETH: *There once was a queen called Matilda.*
Who escaped through the snow – bet that chilled 'er.
Her enemy, Stephen,
Was keen to get even.
If he'd caught her he'd surely have killed 'er…
Boom! Boom!

HENRY: Henry II next…

(HENRY *replaces* MARY *on throne.*)

HENRY: He had terrible trouble with his wife and sons. He gave his friend Thomas à Becket the job as Archbishop of Canterbury, then they argued. Some of his knights murdered Becket because they thought that's what the king wanted.

ELIZABETH: (*sings*) "I am sorry," said old Henry,
"That my old pal Tom is dead.
You knights were really silly to go
bashing in his head.
'Cos Tom was quite a nice guy. If you
had to take a life,
You could have had a chop or two at my
three sons and wife!"

ALL: *'Cos Tom was quite a nice guy. If you*
had to take a life,
You could have had a chop or two at his
three sons and wife!"

(JAMES *replaces* HENRY *on the throne.*)

MARY: Next was Richard I – Lion-heart … but chicken-brain. Got himself captured and cost the English a

27

fortune to pay for his freedom.

JAMES: And he was never in England…

ELIZABETH: (*sings*) *Richard, strong and lion-hearted,*
Was from England often parted.
Spent his life in places sunny.
Still the English gave the money
To release him. Ain't life funny?

(EDWARD *replaces* JAMES *on the throne.*)

CATHERINE: Then there was John. Big, bad John. He was such a rotten king that no other king was ever named after him!

(EDWARD *and* CATHERINE *alternate lines of the next verse.*)

EDWARD: *First John, last John,*
CATHERINE: *John One, only one,*
EDWARD: *Never had another John.*
CATHERINE: *John One, only one,*
EDWARD: *'Cos of all the things he done.*
CATHERINE: *John One, only one.*
HENRY: (*snatches crown and nudges* EDWARD *off throne*) *Henry Three was just as bad*
As the last king, John, his dad.
John, at least, did not last long,
But Henry Three went on and on and on
and on and on and on…

MARY: (*pushes* HENRY *off throne and* EDWARD *back on*) Edward the First hated the Scots so much he wanted his corpse boiled so his bones could be carried into battle after his death!

EDWARD: Horrible!

HENRY: Let's try it on our Edward, shall we?

ELIZABETH: Stop picking on him Henry.

HENRY: *Edward hated every Scot;*
Went to fight them quite a lot.
Dying, he said…

EDWARD: *…tell you what,*
Put my body in a pot;
Boil it up so nice and hot;
Take my bones out, they won't rot,
Won't go mouldy, turn to grot;
Every time you fight the Scot!
Take me with you, fail me not.

HENRY: *Then he died and thot was thot.*

MARY: (*reading*) Urrrgh! Look at what they did to the next king, Edward the Second! They murdered him with a red-hot poker up his bum!

HENRY: Yeah! Let's try it!

ELIZABETH: Then there was Edward III! Started a war against the French that went on for a hundred and sixteen years!

CATHERINE: What was that war called, then?

ELIZABETH: The Hundred Years War, of course.

HENRY: How many Edwards are there?

JAMES: Eight. And eight Henries.

HENRY: Good!

ELIZABETH: (*angry*) That's what I hate about history. It's all about men and battles and killing. What about the poor? What about the women?

CATHERINE: Yeah! What about people like us?

JAMES: You were down-trodden for nearly three hundred years after the Normans landed. I suppose you deserve it really.

HENRY: You tell her, James!

JAMES: Of course the best thing that happened to peasants like *you*…

CATHERINE: Me?

JAMES: Peasants like *you* … was the plague known as the Black Death!

MARY: How could the plague be *good*?

JAMES: I'll show you. The Normans brought a new way of life to England. A sort of human pyramid. (*Jumps on to stage block*) At the top of the pyramid was the king and then his queen. (*He raises* ELIZABETH *to his side*) Then his nobles and landowners. (HENRY *and* MARY *stand sullenly below the block looking up*) And at the bottom were the peasants. (EDWARD, WILL *and* CATHERINE *kneel below them*) You do all the work!

MISS GAME: But the Black Death changed everything. It was carried by fleas on plague rats … though the people of the Measly Middle Ages didn't know that! But they *did* know it was dangerous to stay in the towns. It was safer to run into the country. An English poet called Chaucer told the story of three people who tried that. Let's act it out…

SCENE FOUR

A play within a play. MARY *is the sharp-witted one,* CATHERINE *the sly one and* EDWARD *the dull one.* HENRY *and* JAMES *play the other roles,* MISS GAME *plays Death, as usual, and* ELIZABETH *narrates.*

ELIZABETH: Three friends decided to flee into the forest to escape the effects of the plague. But no one cheats Death.

MARY: (*collapses, panting*) We've run far enough. Let's rest here for the night.

CATHERINE: You think we're safe from Death, Mary?

MARY: Safe as we can be. They say that Death walks the streets in a black hooded cloak. He sweeps you down with his scythe when it's your turn to go.

EDWARD: Your turn to go where, Mary?

31

MARY: To the Land of Death, stupid.

CATHERINE: He must be busy since this plague arrived. Run off his feet!

MARY: He likes it that way. The plague is his friend.

CATHERINE: My husband died of the plague. First he got swellings is his groin and armpit, oozing blood and pus.

MARY: (*agreeing*) Swelling comes first.

CATHERINE: Then he started spitting blood!

MARY: Spitting comes next.

CATHERINE: Then he started to smell dreadfully!

MARY: Smelling is next, and then you hear the swishing of Death's scythe!

EDWARD: Swell – spit – smell – swish!

MARY: (*sniffs at* EDWARD *and edges away*) There's no cure!

CATHERINE: I've heard there are *lots* of cures! The rich eat crushed emeralds but the poor just open a vein and let some blood out. Eating arsenic's another cure!

MARY: In my uncle's village they killed all the cats and dogs.

EDWARD: My mum says you should shave a chicken's bottom and put it against the plague spot!

MARY: Yeah, there are lots of *cures* ... but none of them *work*.

EDWARD: Swell – spit – smell – swish!

MARY: You're stupid, Edward.

EDWARD: (*to audience*) She's just jealous 'cos she can't say it!

(MARY *tries to say this but it turns out to be a tongue-twister. The audience are invited to try it at ever-increasing speed. Finally* EDWARD *stops them.*)

EDWARD: No, listen. It's easier if you sing this little song. (*He teaches audience response while* MARY *and* CATHERINE *dance crazily to it.*)
First you feel a little poorly, then you
   start to swell. (*Raspberry sound.*)
Then you start to spit some blood, and
   then you really smell. Pong!
Time for friends to start to ring your
   fu-ne-ral bell. Dong!
Then along comes nasty Death and
   swishes you to Hell! Gone!

(*On the last round* MARY *and* CATHERINE *collapse in fear while* MISS GAME, *as Death, appears behind the uncomprehending* EDWARD. *"He's behind you" sequence till* EDWARD *finally sees him and hides behind the women.*)

CATHERINE: Sorry! Sorry! Sorry! We wasn't making fun of you.

MARY: Hey! Are you Death?

MISS GAME: (*as Death, pointing to box*) You will find Death underneath that tree.

MARY: Edward! Dig under that tree!

EDWARD: Why me?

MARY: Because you're stupid!

EDWARD: Oh! Right! And if we can kill Death we'll be heroes!

(*The women look on nervously as* EDWARD *unearths a box, while* MISS GAME, *as Death, disappears in the shadows.* ELIZABETH *narrates.*)

ELIZABETH: The box was full of gold. More gold than they'd ever seen in their lives!

MARY: Go back to the village and buy us some wine to celebrate, Edward.

EDWARD: I may catch the plague! Why should I go?

CATHERINE: Because you're stupid.

EDWARD: Oh, all right!

ELIZABETH: But while Edward was gone the other two eyed the gold greedily.

MARY: We're rich.

CATHERINE: We're rich ... but we'd be richer if we had Edward's share.

MARY: He'd kill us.

CATHERINE: Not if we killed him first!

(EDWARD *takes wine bottle from* HENRY. *Mimes drinking some, pouring liquid from second bottle into wine and replacing cork.*)

ELIZABETH: And when Edward returned with the wine that's just what they did!

(*Stylized knifing of* EDWARD *who crawls towards pile of gold before dying.*)

MARY: Give me that wine. I hated doing that. (*She drinks and coughs*) Strong stuff.

CATHERINE: Let me taste. (*Snatches bottle and coughs as* MARY *falls clutching at stomach.*)

MARY: Poison! He poisoned the wine to get his hands on our share of the gold. (*Crawls towards pile of gold but dies as her hand touches it.*)

CATHERINE: (*falls, dying*) Who'd have thought stupid Edward had it in him? (*Falls, clutching at gold*)

(MISS GAME, *as Death, enters and scoops up the box.*)

MISS GAME: (*as Death*) I told them they'd find death underneath that tree.

(*Lights change back to classroom.* HENRY, JAMES, ELIZABETH *and* WILL *applaud. Audience encouraged to join in. All — except* MARY — *rise and bow.*)

SCENE FIVE

EDWARD: You can get up now, Mary. It was only a story.

HENRY: Was it? What did she drink?

EDWARD: Water.

HENRY: (*waves smaller bottle*) But there was *poison* in *this* bottle! You poisoned Mary, Edward! (*Sings*)
Time for friends to start to ring your
fu-ne-ral bell. Dong!
Then along comes nasty Death and
swishes you to Hell! Gone!

EDWARD: No!

CATHERINE: Then he must have poisoned me too!

(*She retches.* HENRY *roars with laughter.*)

HENRY: Only a joke! Get up Mary.

(MARY *doesn't move.* HENRY *walks over to her and shakes her gently.*)

36

HENRY: Mary? Mary!

MARY: (*rolling over suddenly and laughing at him while he staggers back*) Only a *joke* Henry.

(*The group is a little shaken.* WILL *plays softly.*)

WILL: Ho-rib-bull Hiss-tor-ree…

MISS GAME: Very amusing, Henry. But can we get on with the story?

JAMES: The human pyramid!

(*Everyone hurries into their "feudal system" positions.* EDWARD, WILL *and* CATHERINE *kneel at bottom.*)

JAMES: After the Black Death had mown the peasants down… (CATHERINE *and* WILL *are scythed by* MISS GAME, *as Death*) …there weren't enough peasants to work the land.

(EDWARD *rises to feet while higher levels cluster round him crying* "Work for me!")

EDWARD: I'll work for myself.

ELIZABETH: I'll pay you well!

WILL: I'll pay you better!

JAMES: I'll give you land of your own.

EDWARD: *(turns to* HENRY *who has his back to them all)* What about you?

HENRY: *(angry)* You've made your point, Miss Game. Can we get out of the Middle Ages? They must have ended some time!

MISS GAME: Well there were a few more kings after Edward III … Richard II, (Sicky Dicky), Henry IV (Itchy Henry).

HENRY: Why "Itchy" Henry?

MISS GAME: Because he had a skin disease that meant his body was covered in spots, his head infested with lice and his eyes red and raw! He had terrible nightmares – probably felt guilty about having Richard II bumped off.

HENRY: Can't we have a *heroic* Henry?

MISS GAME: Yes! Henry V, his son. Brilliant soldier.

HENRY: That's more like it.

MISS GAME: Followed by Henry VI – Henry Halfwit.

HENRY: You what?

MISS GAME: Murdered in the Tower by Edward IV! He was replaced by the last king of the Middle Ages, his brother, Richard III. Historians…

ALL: *Groan!*

MISS GAME: …*historians* usually say the Middle Ages ended in 1485. The last great battle of knights in England – Bosworth Field. The last king to die in battle – Richard III!

(*The class begin to re-form as they were for the Battle of Hastings, but* EDWARD *is on top as Richard III, and* HENRY *at the bottom as Henry Tudor.*)

MISS GAME: The last great charge of knights!

WILL: Up the hill to death … just like Hastings?

MISS GAME: No! It was a charge *down* the hill that finished Richard III off. He sat there on Ambien Hill at the battle of Bosworth Field. He led the charge down!

WILL: No! He couldn't! Not *again*! Didn't he know what happened to Harold in 1066? (*To* EDWARD, *as Richard III at his side*) Stay on the hilltop! He'll never be able to defeat us while we stay on the hilltop!

MISS GAME: But history repeats itself, they say. (EDWARD *climbs on to* WILL*'s back*) His enemy, a pretender from Wales, jumped on his horse … and charged at the king. Richard was dragged off his horse and cut to pieces!

HENRY: (*as Henry Tudor*) Kill him! Strip him! And bring me his crown!

(*Stylized killing of* EDWARD *as Richard III, and transfer of crown to* HENRY *as Henry Tudor.*)

JAMES: So the Middle Ages ended like they began? With a stupid, *stupid* charge down a hill and a dead king?

ELIZABETH: And a whole new family on the throne.

HENRY: (*snatches book from her and reads it gleefully*) And look at the king's name! Guess what it was?

ALL: Henry?

HENRY: That's me. Henry Tudor.

JAMES: The first of the *terrible* Tudors.

HENRY: (*as Henry Tudor*) Just watch who you're calling terrible, mate, or I'll have your head off!

JAMES: (*to audience*) See what I mean?

SCENE SIX

ELIZABETH: The people of the south of England were pleased to see Henry VII. They reckoned a Welsh king was better than that Richard III with his ruffians from northern England. There's no accounting for tastes!

CATHERINE: (*begins to sing "Cwm Rhondda"*)
Guide us Henry, King of Wales,
Please be King of England, do!
Welcome to our crown and to our throne,
Welcome to our money too!

ALL: *Strong deliverer, strong deliverer,*
Take our cash, take all you need – till we
* bleed,*
Take our cash, take all you need!

MARY: Henry not only took the taxes. He also took the niece of Richard III as a wife! Princess Elizabeth became Queen Elizabeth.

ELIZABETH: (*to "We'll keep a welcome in the hillside"*)
I guess I'll have to marry Henry,
Though he's a weed and he's so mean.
It will bring re-con-ci-li-ation
And after all, he'll make me queen.

HENRY: *We will have lots of little Tudors,*
And we will reign a thousand years.

WILL: *And when the babies all start crying*
Then he'll come home again to wails!
(*Stops singing to explain*) Crying? Wailing? Come home to *wails*? Geddit? Oh, never mind. (*He is shouted down.*)

JAMES: Henry never felt safe on the English throne. Even with Richard III dead there were still rivals. There was the son of Edward IV – the young, kind Edward V.

(EDWARD *staggers forward – terrified. The lights fade till he is isolated.* MISS GAME, *as Death, stands behind him.*)

41

JAMES: It was widely believed that Richard III had put prince Edward in the Tower of London and then had him smothered to death. (EDWARD *turns, sees Death, and screams*) But others believe Edward V was still alive when Henry Tudor reached the Tower of London!

HENRY: (*as Henry Tudor, stepping into light*) Edward! How good to see you!

EDWARD: (*as Edward V*) Who are you?

HENRY: (*as Henry Tudor*) Henry Tudor – now King Henry VII.

EDWARD: (*as Edward V*) You can't be king! While I'm alive I'm the rightful King of England.

HENRY: (*as Henry Tudor*) True!

EDWARD: (*as Edward V*) But if you set me free, Henry Tudor, I'll let *you* be king of Wales. It's your home, after all.

HENRY: (*as Henry Tudor, singing softly*)
Oh land of my fathers, the land of the free,
The home of the Telyn, so soothing to me;
Thy noble descenders were gallant and brave
For freedom their heart's life they gave.

(EDWARD, *as Edward V, joins him.*)

EDWARD: ⎫ *Wales, Wales, home sweet home is Wales.*
HENRY: ⎬ *Till death be passed, my love shall last,*

My longing, my yearning for Wales.

(HENRY *clicks his fingers and* MISS GAME, *as Death, smothers* EDWARD. HENRY *rises to his feet and places a foot on* EDWARD's *body while the others gather round him. They join in the chorus.*)

ALL: *Wales, Wales, home sweet home is Wales. Till death be passed, our love shall last…*

(*Sudden silence.* HENRY *finishes softly.*)

HENRY: *…But England is richer than Wales.*

(HENRY *takes backslaps and bows. The others adapt costumes.* ELIZABETH *and* CATHERINE *step forward.* WILL *plays the theme, "Ho-rib-bull Hiss-tor-ree, why we have to learn it's a miss-tor-ree!"*)

CATHERINE: It must be wonderful being a queen of a country like England!

ELIZABETH: (*as Elizabeth of York*) Henry Tudor's teeth are bad and his breath is worse. He is so tight-fisted he makes me patch my dresses and wear tin buckles on my shoes instead of silver.

CATHERINE: That's shocking that is, Elizabeth.

ELIZABETH: (*as Elizabeth of York*) Ah, but we do have some fine children. I gave him his heir!

WILL: (*as Prince Arthur, steps forward*) I didn't know he was bald!

ELIZABETH: (*as Elizabeth of York*) Heir, not hair. Heir to the throne, dummy. Our son, Prince Arthur.

HENRY: (*as Henry Tudor, to* WILL) I hereby make you Prince of Wales!

ALL: Hooray!

ELIZABETH: (*as Elizabeth of York*) But our poor little Arthur married Catherine of Aragon … and then fell sick.

(MISS GAME, *as Death, steps forward and claims* WILL *– he falls.*)

WILL: (*as Prince Arthur, dying*) That's life. Heir today and gone tomorrow. (*Dies.*)

ELIZABETH: (*as Elizabeth of York*) I guess that makes little Henry Junior our heir!

(HENRY *quickly changes and drops on to knees, stuffs chicken leg into mouth – speaks in baby voice*)

HENRY: I'll be Henry the Ate!

ELIZABETH: (*as Elizabeth of York, bends down*

	towards him) The *eighth*!
HENRY:	(*as Henry VIII, tries to articulate "eighth" and spits chicken in her face*) Eight-th-th-th.
ELIZABETH:	(*as Elizabeth of York*) I'll marry Henry off to Catherine of Aragon. (CATHERINE *smiles down on* HENRY *and takes his hand*) And my daughter, Margaret (MARY *steps forward*), we'll marry her off to the Stuart king of Scotland!
MARY:	(*as Margaret, outraged*) Scotland! Oh, Mum! You know what they say about the Scots! They're so *mean*!
WILL:	(*jumps up*) I say, I say, I say! The Scots were so mean they went to Margaret's wedding and had confetti on elastic! They're so mean they keep their clocks in a bank because they want to save time!
ALL:	Shut up!
MARY:	(*as Margaret, angry*) My heirs will be back!
JAMES:	Of course Henry VII died and his son became Henry VIII.

SCENE SEVEN

Flashing lights and fanfare.

JAMES:	(*with red book under his arm*) Henry the

Eighth, king of England, "This is your Wife!"

HENRY: *(as Henry VIII)* Which one?

JAMES: Your sixth wife, Catherine Parr! Come on in, Catherine!

(CATHERINE *enters as Catherine Parr.*)

CATHERINE: *(as Catherine Parr)* Hello, love.

JAMES: Now, Catherine, you are Henry's *sixth* wife. Aren't you afraid you'll go the same way as all the rest?

CATHERINE: *(as Catherine Parr)* No, James, you see I have a special friend to protect me. My friend Death!

HENRY: *(as Henry VIII)* Death is my friend too! Death may get *you* before it gets *me*!

CATHERINE: *(as Catherine Parr)* We'll have to wait and see, Henry dear.

JAMES: Yes, Henry Tudor, Death has been a constant companion throughout your life.

MARY: *(as Mary Tudor, voice off)* And the first victim was my mother!

JAMES: Come on in, Mary Tudor, and tell us about your father!

(MARY *enters as Mary Tudor.*)

MARY: *(as Mary Tudor)* Catherine of Aragon

married Henry and I was born. But
she failed to give him a son and heir.
So he rejected her and took up with a
new love, Anne Boleyn.

ELIZABETH: (*as Elizabeth Tudor, voice off*) And that
was *my* mother!

JAMES: Come on in, Elizabeth Tudor!

(ELIZABETH *enters as Elizabeth Tudor.*)

MARY: (*as Mary Tudor, furious*) *Your* mother,
Anne Boleyn, had *my* mother poisoned!

ELIZABETH: (*as Elizabeth Tudor*) That's just a story,
my ugly half-sister. And poisoning was
kind compared to what our father did
to the others.

JAMES: That's right! First Henry tried to
divorce Catherine. When the Pope
refused Henry abolished the Catholic
Church and made himself head of a
Protestant Church of England.

MARY: (*as Mary Tudor*) He divorced my
mother and left her to die in misery.

WILL: (*voice off*) And whoever tried to oppose
him was executed. Monks were hanged
from the steeples of their churches.
Peasants were hanged from the windows
of their own homes in front of their
wives and children. Honest lords like

47

Thomas More were beheaded.

ELIZABETH: (*as Elizabeth Tudor*) And, when my mother couldn't give him the son he wanted he had *her* beheaded!

EDWARD: (*as Edward Tudor, voice off*) That's right! He married my mother.

JAMES: Yes, Henry, you married Jane Seymour and she gave you the son you always wanted … Edward Tudor!

(EDWARD *enters, as Edward Tudor. Holds out hands to* HENRY. *He rejects him.*)

HENRY: (*as Henry VIII*) Jane died giving birth to that boy. The only woman I ever loved! (*Children jeer at him.*)

JAMES: You married wife number four after seeing her picture! But when you met her you were in for a shock!

(WILL *enters under a veil, as Anne of Cleeves.* HENRY *lifts veil and* WILL *pulls grotesque face.*)

JAMES: You divorced Anne of Cleeves like a shot. You were getting fat and ugly and smelly by now but you married a nineteen-year-old girl. Catherine Howard.

48

(CATHERINE *appears as Catherine Howard before being bungled off to execution.*)

JAMES: What did you do when you found you weren't her first boyfriend?

HENRY: (*as Henry VIII*) She betrayed me!

JAMES: What did *you* do?

HENRY: (*as Henry VIII*) Sentenced her to death! She asked for it!

JAMES: The young queen screamed and begged you for mercy. You turned a deaf ear and sent her to the block, didn't you?

HENRY: (*as Henry VIII*) So what?

JAMES: So you married wife number six. Catherine Parr.

CATHERINE: (*as Catherine Parr*) He even came close to having me executed! But my friend saved me.

JAMES: Henry. Overweight, with oozing sores on your legs that refused to heal, hardly able to walk. At last Catherine's friend came for you. Death!

HENRY: (*as Henry VIII*) I'm not ready to go! I'm only fifty-five.

CATHERINE: (*as Catherine Parr*) Never mind, love … we'll all miss you. (*To* HENRY's *children*) Won't we?

ALL: No!

(Death strikes HENRY *down. Suddenly the lights dim. Then they come up and we are back in the classroom.* MINDE'*s voice booms out.)*

MINDE: *(voice)* It is getting close to break-time. I will return by the end of next lesson to test you. I hope you're ready to be tested! I will release four of you from the classroom during break. Three must stay as my hostages.

MARY: *(to* MISS GAME*)* We're not ready to be tested, Miss, are we? How will your drama help us now?

MISS GAME: Let's try a little role play. You all know your parts. We have Edward as Edward VI, you Mary as Mary I and Elizabeth as Elizabeth I … the last three Tudors. All you have to do is study *one* of the characters over break – then test one another!

WILL: *(looking to audience)* Can't we use some of the kids in the corridor to do a sort of mock exam?

MISS GAME: If you can find two teams willing to do it.

WILL: *(to audience)* You will help us, won't you? Look, if you do well we'll give you a free copy of this history book. *(Holds up "The Mad Millennium".)*

HENRY: And if they fail … well, it won't hurt
           them *very* much, will it?

JAMES: Well, not an *awful* lot. Not as much as
           having your finger nails torn out or
           being eaten alive by piranha fish.

WILL: (*at keyboard*) *Ho-rib-bull Hiss-tor-ee,*
                why we have to learn it's a miss-tor-ee!

ALL: *Ho-rib-bull Hiss-tor-ee, why we have to*
                learn it's a miss-tor-ee.

HENRY: *The Tudors were cruel with their*
                torturing tools.
           But this history is worse when it makes us
                look fools!

ALL: *Ho-rib-bull Hiss-tor-ree, why we have to*
                learn it's a miss-tor-ee!

           (*A bell rings.*)

MISS GAME: Right! Breaktime. Edward, Mary and
           Elizabeth, study the books. James and
           Catherine, help Will, Henry and me to
           find some volunteers.

HENRY: (*sadly*) I still say they look thick!

INTERVAL

51

ACT TWO

SCENE EIGHT

The characters hurry back into the room with
ELIZABETH, HENRY, EDWARD *and* MARY *still dressed*
as their Tudor monarch name-sakes. JAMES *plays*
quiz-show host and two teams of 3–4 children are lined
up on either side. WILL *helps one side and* CATHERINE
the other. There is a scoreboard in the middle.

JAMES: Good evening boys and girls, ladies
and gentlemen … and teachers.
Welcome to the new quiz show …
Murder That Monarch! (*Applause*)
Now I'm sure you all know the rules.
Answer the questions correctly and
your monarch stays alive, and *you* win
a fabulous trip to a museum! (*Audience
whipped up to ecstasy at this
announcement!*) Get one wrong and
the monarch dies. Here is my lovely
assistant, Catherine, to introduce the
contestants!

CATHERINE: Well, James, on our right we have
children from school "X" (*cheers*) who
have to look after King Henry VIII
and his daughter Mary I. On our left
we have children from school "Y"

52

(*cheers*) who have to look after Henry's two younger children, Edward VI and Elizabeth I.

JAMES: Now, King Henry, (HENRY *sits on "throne" centre stage*) can you tell us your hobbies?

HENRY: (*as Henry VIII*) Eating, women and hunting.

JAMES: Look out, girls! King Henry likes eating women! Now, on with the game! First question to your highness.

HENRY: (*as Henry VIII*) My wife Anne Boleyn used to go to feasts, eat and then throw up all she'd just eaten. She had two ladies-in-waiting to hold up a white sheet while she vomited at the table. Is that true or false?

(*Answer: true. Team "X" answer. If they get it wrong then* HENRY *is zapped by a flashing light and claimed by* MISS GAME, *as Death. If they get it right then* HENRY *asks an "impossible" follow up till they get it wrong, for example, "What were the names of the ladies-in-waiting?"*)

JAMES: Yes, Henry VIII wrote the song "Whitesleeves" for his wife Anne.

53

	Then she threw up and he changed the song to "Greensleeves"!
WILL:	(*sings*) *Alas, my love, you are looking bad. Perhaps it's the mouldy old peas you had. I used to love your white dress, it's sad, Because since you've been sick it's got Green sleeves.*
JAMES:	Let's move along to the team from "Y". Edward VI, ask your horrible historical question!
EDWARD:	(*as Edward VI*) I was a sickly youth and fell ill with consumption. My body swelled up, my hair dropped out and then my fingers began to turn black and drop off! True or false?

(*Answer: true. Team "Y" are questioned till they get something wrong, for example, "What happened to the fingers that fell off?", and* EDWARD *is zapped*)

JAMES:	Yes, King Ed died at the age of just 15, in agony, with his fingers dropping off. There was no cure!
WILL:	I say, James.
JAMES:	Yes, Will?
WILL:	He should have gone to a second-hand shop!
JAMES:	If you don't mind, I'll tell the jokes

and get the laughs on this show! Now with Eddie deadie his big sister Mary took the throne. Mary Tudor, Catholic fanatic with an illness that made her breath stink! (*Encourages audience to react with "Poo!"*) What are your hobbies, Mary?

MARY: (*as Mary I*) Having Protestants burned to death, James!

JAMES: Yes, folks, it's cheaper than coal! Hah! Hah! Now, Mary, ask your question.

MARY: (*as Mary I*) I was a gentle and tender queen. When I had those Protestants burned I made their death quick and painless. I had gunpowder strapped to their bodies so they would be blown to bits and die quickly! Aren't I kind?

(*Answer: "yes" or "no" – either is wrong. MARY is zapped.*)

JAMES: Well, team "X" this is your last chance to win a fabulous trip to a museum.

WILL: It's the *Museum Of Kind-hearted Teachers* – it's a very *small* museum! Hah!

JAMES: It's your turn Elizabeth, Queen of England! (ELIZABETH *takes the chair*) Now, Good Queen Bess, tell us a little about yourself!

ELIZABETH: (*as Elizabeth I*) I am a Protestant. All the Protestants that Misery Mary burned will become saints! And any Catholics will be punished.

JAMES: In fact, in York, you had a Catholic woman placed under a huge weight and crushed to death, didn't you?

ELIZABETH: (*as Elizabeth I*) She refused to confess.

WILL: After being crushed she *flatly* refused!

JAMES: And your cousin, Mary Queen of Scots begged you to shelter her from her revolting people.

ELIZABETH: (*as Elizabeth I*) And I gave her shelter but she plotted to take my throne!

JAMES:- So what did you do?

ELIZABETH: (*as Elizabeth I*) I had her beheaded! (*Turns to team "Y"*) And that's my question. When Mary Queen of Scots was beheaded, it took three chops to get her head off? True or false?

(*Answer: true*)

JAMES: That's right. The executioner nicked her with the first chop. Hacked her with the second and needed to do a bit of sawing to get through the gristle. Then when he picked up the head he found Mary had been wearing a wig –

the head fell out and bounced over the
scaffold! True or false, team "Y"?

(*Answer: true, the head slipped; but false
because heads don't bounce, they go splat!
Either way the team get it wrong.*
ELIZABETH *is zapped.*)

CATHERINE: Oh, dear! Neither team have won
tonight's star prize. So push off back
to your schools and learn a bit of
history!

JAMES: But give our losers a great big round
of applause, folks!

(*Teams leave the stage. Characters relax
and take off costumes.*)

MARY: Hey! That was fun!

(*All agree. Then* MISS GAME *pushes the
button on the tape and the booming voice
of* MINDE *interrupts them.*)

MINDE: Fun? Fun! You aren't *here* to have *fun*.
You have just half an hour to cover the
last four hundred years of history.
Then you will be tested. You may
enjoy tormenting those poor children

with your silly games, but just wait
until you are sitting in the chair and I
am asking the questions. You won't
think it's "fun" then, I can promise
you. Now start at the Stuarts and stop
slacking.

EDWARD: What do we do, Miss?

MISS GAME: What he says, I suppose. Look at the
highlights from the Stuarts.

SCENE NINE

EDWARD: Were they Welsh too, Miss?

MISS GAME: No, Edward. They were Scottish.

WILL: From Scotland.

MISS GAME: James Stuart came down from
Scotland to take the English throne.
(JAMES *adopts role of James I*) Here,
Mary, read what a French visitor said
about him.

MARY: (*reads while* JAMES *enacts description
grotesquely and others react*) "James was
of middle height, more fat because of
his clothes than his body. His clothes
always being made large and easy, the
doublets quilted to be dagger-proof.
His breeches were in great pleats and
full stuffed. He was naturally timid,

his eyes large and always rolling after any stranger came into his presence. His beard was very thin. His tongue too large for his mouth which made him drink very badly as if eating his drink which came out into the cup from each side of his mouth."

MISS GAME: And he forgot to mention that James picked his nose and used his sleeve instead of a handkerchief! He was also drunk most of the time. But he was determined to be a strong king. When he arrived at Newark he showed his power.

JAMES: (*as James I, with drunken Scottish accent*) I would like to say how lucky you are to have me for your king. (*Scuffle among watchers*) What's going on there?

(HENRY *drags* EDWARD *forward.*)

HENRY: It's a pickpocket, your highness.

JAMES: A pockpicket! (*spraying words in* HENRY*'s face. Turns to* MARY *who is Queen Anne at his side and sprays her too*) A pockpicket!

MARY: (*as Queen Anne*) Let's just call him a "thief", shall we?

JAMES: (*as James I, spraying words worse than ever*) A th-th-th-thief! I'll no be having no pockpicketing th-th-thiefs in my country. Hang him!

HENRY: But…

JAMES: (*as James I*) *Hang* the villain.

(HENRY *bows and leads* EDWARD *off. There is a strangled cry and then silence.*)

HENRY: It is done your majesty … but there is one thing I should like to mention.

JAMES: (*as James I*) What's that?

HENRY: You're not in Scotland now. The king of England doesn't have the right to hang a man without a trial!

JAMES: (*as James I*) Oh yes I do!

HENRY: Oh, no you don't!

JAMES: (*as James I*) Oh, yes I do!

MARY: (*as Queen Anne*) Oh, no you don't!

JAMES: (*as James I*) I don't?

MARY: (*as Queen Anne*) You don't.

JAMES: (*as James I*) Ah, well, tell the man I'm sorry and I pardon him!

HENRY: But he's dead!

JAMES: (*as James I*) Tell him anyway. (*Slumps on to throne*) He's lucky. Up in Scotland we used to torture criminals before they died. I was specially fond

60

of watching witches being tortured
and burned. Have you no got any
witches you want trying?

HENRY: Sorry, your Majesty. We do have a
plotter, though.

JAMES: (*as James I*) A plotter! (*Spitting his "p"
words as usual*) What's his name?

HENRY: A man called Guy Fawkes, your majesty.
He was caught laying gunpowder under
the Houses of Parliament.

JAMES: (*as James I*) They plotted against me
in Scotland, you know. Plotters! I'm
surrounded by plotters!

MARY: (*as Queen Anne*) Let's show these
English what you did with plotters,
Jamie darling.

(*She takes microphone and narrates as if
for a fashion show.* MISS GAME *is the
torturer and* EDWARD *the victim.* JAMES
watches and cheers. ELIZABETH *and*
CATHERINE *look on in disgust.*)

MARY: (*as Queen Anne*) First we have the
wonderful Piniewinks! Yes, these little
screws attach to the thumbs and are
tightened until they bleed! Now let's
look at the lovely Cashielaws – an iron
case around the leg which is slowly

heated up. And Guy Fawkes here is modelling the latest in the Boot – an iron foot-crusher. The harder the wedges are hammered in the more the pain. Finally the delightful Heid rope – a knotted rope, placed round the skull and wound tighter.

EDWARD: Let me die!

(MISS GAME *drags him off*. MARY *comforts him while* CATHERINE, EDWARD *and* ELIZABETH *move downstage*.)

ELIZABETH: He's an animal.
CATHERINE: A beast.
ELIZABETH: I'll be glad when he's dead!
MISS GAME: (*stands in front of* JAMES *and announces*) The king is dead. Long live the king!

(MISS GAME *steps aside to reveal* JAMES *who has become Charles I*.)

ELIZABETH: Charles I – James's son!
CATHERINE: Another little Scot with a squeaky voice and a stammer.
JAMES: (*as Charles I*) I am your k-k-k-king!
CATHERINE: Ooooh! He's our k-k-k-king!
JAMES: (*as Charles I*) I am God's m-m-minister on Earth!

(*The others gather round him in a hostile manner. They jeer.*)

HENRY:	I thought God was an Englishman!
MARY:	Or an English woman!
JAMES:	(*as Charles I*) You will accept my Catholic wife!
ALL:	No!
JAMES:	(*as Charles I*) And you will worship the way I tell you!
ALL:	(*furious*) Never!
HENRY:	We're Puritans and want to worship as Puritans, don't we? We'll form an army and throw the King off the throne!
WILL:	He'll be *really* "thrown" then, won't he?
JAMES:	(*as Charles I*) W-w-w-wait! I will call on my loyal Scots to fight for me!

(*Mob goes silent and huddles at front of stage.*)

HENRY:	Scotland's a foreign country. What is it if you encourage a foreign army to invade?
WILL:	Treason!
MARY:	And what's the punishment for treason?
ELIZABETH:	Hanging by the neck till he's almost dead, drawing his guts out of his body

and burning them in front of his very eyes, then cutting his body into quarters.

CATHERINE: Yeah! That's what his dad did to Guy Fawkes.

EDWARD: Excuse me. But Charles is a noble.

HENRY: So what?

EDWARD: So a noble has the right to be executed by beheading.

HENRY: Oh, all right. Parliament will have a vote on it. All those against?

ELIZABETH: Sixty-seven!

HENRY: All those in favour?

ELIZABETH: Sixty-eight!

(*They grab* JAMES, *as Charles I, and drag him up on a stage block.*)

JAMES: (*as Charles I, whispers*) I die a Christian of the Church of England.

(*Mob surrounds him.*)

WILL: Shout up, mate! They can't hear you at the back. (*To audience*) Can you? And you want to hear the famous last words, don't you?

JAMES: (*as Charles I*) I die a Christian of the Church of England. I will say no more.

(MISS GAME *enters with an executioner's*
mask and a headsman's axe as they
gather round the block)

JAMES: (*as Charles I*) Remember!
CATHERINE: Remember? Remember what?
WILL: I don't know! I've forgot!

(*As they close around the execution scene*
the axe comes down. There is a stunned
silence and a shudder runs through the
group. HENRY *reaches forward and*
snatches the dummy severed head and
shows it to the audience.)

HENRY: Behold the head of a traitor!

(*They throw the head from one to*
another then begin a celebratory country
dance – MISS GAME *stops them abruptly.*)

MISS GAME: This country is now run by Puritans.
Common dancing will stop!
HENRY: Let's go to the theatre!
MISS GAME: The theatres have all been closed.
MARY: Oh, Christmas!
MISS GAME: Christmas will no longer be
celebrated.
EDWARD: But Father Christmas…

MISS GAME: Father Christmas is dead.

CATHERINE: Oh, Hell!

MISS GAME: And swearing will be punished by a flogging and a spell in prison. Now, give me the king's head.

EDWARD: What are you going to do with it?

MISS GAME: Stitch it back on to the body so he can be given a respectable burial.

WILL: Can we give him a good send off with…

MISS GAME: No! there will be no singing or dancing or feasting with the funeral. Get back to work!

SCENE TEN

The characters sit gloomily around the stage.

HENRY: Bore-ring. Boring, boring, boring!

CATHERINE: I agree, Henry. I mean kings were cruel and queens were mean…

HENRY: But they were never bore-ring, were they?

MISS GAME: Well, the Protector, Oliver Cromwell died, of course. So, what do you want? Another Protector? Or another king?

JAMES: Would it be possible to have a king … but a king with no real power over the people?

MISS GAME: You can have King Charles!

EDWARD: What? With his head stitched back on?

MISS GAME: No. Charles the Second – his son!

CATHERINE: That'll be fun!

HENRY: (*jumps on to rostrum*) Yes! I'm Charles II the Merry Monarch!

ALL: Hooray!

CATHERINE: Cheerful Charlie! What have you got for us?

HENRY: (*as Charles II*) After three hundred boring years I bring you … the Great Plague!

ALL: Hooray! (*They sing and dance at double speed*)
    First you feel a little poorly, then you
        start to swell. (*Raspberry sound*.)
    Then you start to spit some blood, and
        then you really smell. Pong!
    Time for friends to start to ring your
        fu-ne-ral bell. Dong!
    Then along comes nasty Death and
        swishes you to Hell! Gone!

HENRY: (*as Charles II*) But before you have a chance to get bored with that, I'll show you an end to the plague!

ELIZABETH: Don't be ridiculous! No one knows a cure for the plague.

HENRY: (*as Charles II*) The plague spreads through the filthy London houses. All we need is a little fire to burn down those houses! I will call this "The Great Fire of London".

MARY: (*narrates as others enact in mime*) The story goes that it was started by a little orphan boy (EDWARD) who was starving hungry. Early one morning he came across a baker's shop in Pudding Lane. The baker (JAMES) had put loaves on the windowsill to cool. As the baker raked hot ashes out of his oven the little boy sneaked a hand up for a loaf. The baker saw him and swung round sharply. The ashes scattered over the wooden floor of his shop and started a fire! Neighbours passed buckets of water in a chain (ALL) but the blaze spread till half of London was ablaze.

HENRY: (*as Charles II*) Pull down houses in the path of the flames! Make a fire-break! And I, your king, will join in the fire-fighting! (*Cheers*) That's it! We're winning!

JAMES: We're not! The fire is simply running out of things to burn!

(*Exhausted characters sink to ground coughing and moaning.*)

HENRY: (*as Charles II*) My people! We will
              rebuild London!

ALL: (*feeble*) Hooray!

HENRY: (*as Charles II*) I hereby award a purse
              of 100 guineas to the fire-fighters!

ALL: (*slightly stronger*) Hooray!

MISS GAME: Not a lot of people know the story of
              the Frenchman. He confessed to
              starting the fire.

EDWARD: (*as Frenchman*) Je confess! I started le
              fire! Je suis guilty! Hang me!

CATHERINE: You hear that? He did it!

ELIZABETH: He couldn't have done! He wasn't even
              in London when the fire started.

CATHERINE: What should we do with him?

MISS GAME: What do you think they did?

HENRY: (*as Charles II*) Hang him anyway!

(MISS GAME, *as Death, takes him away.
There is a strangled cry and the rest
cheer. The characters sit tiredly on the
ground.*)

CATHERINE: Plagues, fires! I told you it was never
              boring with kings around! Whatever
              next?

(HENRY, MARY, WILL *and* ELIZABETH
move around throne like musical chairs.)

69

MARY:	Revolution! Charles died...
HENRY:	What?
MARY:	Charles died.
HENRY:	Oh, that's not fair.
MARY:	And his brother James II took over. But he was a secret Catholic.
ALL:	Boo!
MARY:	So there was a Glorious Revolution and his daughter (*points at herself*) Mary took over – with my dearly beloved hubby, William. (WILL *joins her.*)
ELIZABETH:	But Mary died of small pox when she was just 32!
MARY:	Aw, come on! I want to be queen!
WILL:	You're dead! Get off the throne. Your husband, William, reigned on!
ELIZABETH:	Till his horse stumbled on a mole-hill, and he fell off and died.
WILL:	Not fair! I haven't been king since the Norman days!
ELIZABETH:	And (*pointing at herself*) Queen Anne took over!
ALL:	Then she died!
MISS GAME:	And that was the end of the Slimy Stuarts!
HENRY:	Who's next?
MISS GAME:	The Gorgeous Georgians, of course.
MARY:	Why do you call them gorgeous?
MISS GAME:	Because of the way they dressed up!

SCENE ELEVEN

MARY:	I wish *we* could dress up.
CATHERINE:	We can! We have the drama box and the stage make-up.
ELIZABETH:	But we are not allowed to wear make-up in school, are we?
MARY:	No, but teachers can!
CATHERINE:	Yeah. That's not fair.
MARY:	I mean we can use a teacher as a model!
JAMES:	Miss Game would do it, wouldn't you, Miss?
MISS GAME:	I couldn't. I've another class after this...
JAMES:	But in the interests of our history education. You don't want us to fail Master Minde's test, do you?
MISS GAME:	No, but...
JAMES:	Then sit in this chair and let's get started!

(*They sit her on "throne" chair which has two clasps on each arm. She is nervous.* JAMES *fastens clasps as* CATHERINE *and* MARY *begin work.* EDWARD *picks up a book and reads while* HENRY *looks on.* WILL *sings as girls do a grotesque make-over.*)

71

WILL:

White is beautiful, dear ladies,
Smear your face with paint of lead;
Never mind the lead has made
The men who mixed it ill ... or dead.
Take some silk of red or black,
Cut a circle or a crescent;
Stick it to your face to cover
Small-pox scars ... it's much more
pleasant
Take some plaster, dyed bright red,
Crush it to a ruby paste;
Smear it on your lips, dear ladies,
Never mind the chalky taste.
Shave your eyebrows clean away,
Take a trap and catch some mice;
Make false eyebrows from the mouse-
skin,
Stick them on to look so nice.
Make your face look sweet and chubby,
Pack your mouth with balls of cork;
Fit your false teeth in the middle,
Hope you don't choke when you talk.
Next you need a monster wig
If you want to look real smashin';
When your wig has reached the ceiling
Then you'll be the "height" of fashion!
Decorate your lovely hair-piece,
Use the feathers of a parrot;
Add some ribbons, fruit and flowers,

From your ears then hang a carrot.
Last of all you'll need a fan
To flutter at your favourite feller;
Now you'll look like Ugly Sister
To the pretty Cinderella!

MARY: Go and look at yourself in a mirror, Miss! There's one on the back of the cupboard door!

(MISS GAME *stumbles to the cupboard and opens the door. She falls into the cupboard and the door slams closed behind her.*)

EDWARD: Somebody help her!

(*He hurries to door, throws it open and is confronted by the roaring image of a monstrous mummy with glowing eyes that terrified* JAMES *in the opening scene.*)

EDWARD: We've lost our teacher!
CATHERINE: Where did she go?
JAMES: I don't know, but I think that Master Minde had something to do with it.
MINDE: (*voice roars*) You are right, young James. And you have just twenty minutes before I return and test you. I hope you have finished by then.

JAMES: (*shouts*) We're up to the Georgians!

MINDE: Shame the Georgians aren't even on the National Curriculum. Hah! Hah! You need to study the Victorians and right up to the end of World War I.

CATHERINE: We haven't got a teacher, sir!

MINDE: That's not my problem!

(*There is a silence and the students look at one another.*)

EDWARD: We could teach ourselves from the books.

HENRY: Yeah, stupid, we *could*. But we need someone to organize us.

ELIZABETH: The way people in history had kings and queens.

HENRY: Exactly.

JAMES: I'm the cleverest. I know the most.

ELIZABETH: And I command the most respect.

HENRY: That's not how Kings like William the Conqueror got power.

WILL: I was William the Conqueror. It should be me!

HENRY: That was *playing*, sunshine. This is for real now. William the Conqueror was king because he was the best fighter, and the toughest man. So I guess that makes me King of the Class! Anyone want to argue? (*Everyone else looks away*) You, Edward, will clean my shoes if I tell you to. And you girls can dance for me if I order you to. And you, James will have your head knocked off if you argue. Have you all got that? I'm the monarch! Where do we start, James?

JAMES: I guess that makes you Queen Victoria!

(*All laugh.*)

HENRY: We are *not* amused! Let's do some *horrible* history instead.

JAMES: There was plenty of that in vile Victorian times. Slums…

ELIZABETH: Forty thousand people in Liverpool lived in cellars.

JAMES: …and disease…

ELIZABETH: Cholera, for example, where people turned blue before they died.

JAMES: …cruel teachers…

HENRY: So nothing much has changed.

JAMES: …and gruesome murders.

ELIZABETH: …Jack the Ripper stalking the streets of London!

MARY: And awful theatre shows where they showed melodramas!

SCENE TWELVE

WILL *plays "Hearts and Flowers" with lots of vibrato as the students prepare to enact the Victorian age as a melodrama.* JAMES *and* EDWARD *act as narrators.*

JAMES: When a baby was born in Victorian times the friends of the family asked…

CATHERINE: (*to* HENRY *and* MARY *as parents of a bundled doll*) Has it come to stay?

HENRY: (*as parent*) We pray to God that it has.

EDWARD: An 1860 report said "In the last five years, in this one London district, at least 278 infants were murdered. More than sixty were found in the River Thames, in canals or ponds, and over a hundred were found under railway arches, on doorsteps, in dust-holes, cellars and the like.

HENRY: (*as parent*) Mary, darling.

MARY: (*as parent*) Yes, Henry, dear light of my life?

HENRY: (*as parent*) How can we best care for this dear sweet child? We are so, so poor.

MARY: (*as parent*) There is a good woman called Margaret Walters who lives in the cottages by the railway and who cares for children for a small fee.

HENRY: (*as parent*) Then let us take our darling babe to her.

(*They take baby to* ELIZABETH, *as* MARGARET WALTERS.)

ELIZABETH: (*as parent*) I am what's known as a baby-farmer. For just five pounds I'll care for your child.

HENRY: (*as parent*) For how long, good woman?

ELIZABETH: (*as Margaret Walters*) Oh, for the rest of its life, dear sir.

MARY: (*as parent*) Then here is my sweet infant. Boo! Hoo! Goodbye! I know I leave you in caring hands!

(*They leave.*)

ELIZABETH: (*as Margaret Walters*) Five pounds for *life* doesn't sound much. But if that life is very *short* then it pays me! Hah! (*Flings baby into a corner.*)

JAMES: Margaret Walters was finally brought to trial for the treatment of one child.

EDWARD: (*picks up bundle*) The report said: "There was scarcely a bit of flesh on the bones. It could only be recognized by the hair. It did not cry, being much too weak for that. It was scarcely human. I mean it looked more like a monkey than a child. It was a shadow."

ELIZABETH: (*as Margaret Walters*) Me? I blame the parents!

JAMES: The baby died.

EDWARD: Margaret Walters was hanged!

HENRY: (*as parent*) We would never have left the dear boy if we had but known!

MARY: (*as parent*) It was a girl, my sweetness!

HENRY: (*as parent*) Whatever! In future we will bring up our own.

MARY: (*as parent*) Where will we get the money to feed our little jewels?

HENRY: (*as parent*) Let them work, my lamb!

JAMES: As soon as a child could crawl they were making matchboxes.

ELIZABETH: (*as child*) Mama! I've made all these boxes of matches. What shall I do now?

MARY: (*as parent*) Why, go out on the street corner and sell them.

ELIZABETH: (*as child*) I have no shoes and it's freezing cold, mama!

MARY: (*as parent*) Then the sooner you sell them the better!

EDWARD: (*as child*) What should I do, Papa?

HENRY: (*as parent*) You my son can be a chimney sweep! Oh, you'll have such fun! You're such a skinny child you'll slip up and down easily. And the kind

	old sweep will give you a sack of soft warm soot to sleep on.
EDWARD:	(*as child*) What if I get stuck, papa?
HENRY:	(*as parent*) Then the jolly old sweep will light a fire underneath you and that'll soon shift you!
EDWARD:	(*as child*) And what if I scrape my elbows and knees?
HENRY:	(*as parent*) Then the dear old sweep will pickle them for you!

(*He grabs* EDWARD *and acts out* JAMES*'s narrative.*)

JAMES:	A Victorian sweep said: "No one knows the cruelty they undergo in learning. The flesh must be hardened. This is done by rubbing the skin with strong salt water, close by a hot fire. You have to stand over them with a cane!"
ELIZABETH:	(*as child*) Is there nothing else we can do?
HENRY:	(*as parent*) Work in the nail factory…
CATHERINE:	Where the punishment for bad work is to have nails hammered through your ears.
HENRY:	(*as parent*) Work in the ribbon factory…
CATHERINE:	Where the whirring machines cause

damage to your brain and your spine and can kill you.

HENRY: (*as parent*) Work in the mines…

CATHERINE: Where little boys sit by the edge of the rail tracks in complete darkness for hours on end to open the doors as trucks come through.

HENRY: (*as parent*) And where the trucks crush them to death if they dare to fall asleep.

CATHERINE: Or end up in the workhouse…

HENRY: (*as parent*) Where there are jobs like bone-picking where you have to scrape the last scraps of meat off bones to make soup.

CATHERINE: And where paupers have been known to fight to the death over a miserable scrap of filthy flesh!

HENRY: (*as parent*) Or work in a spinning factory for ten hours a day and be belted with a strap for five minutes if you are caught with a window open.

CATHERINE: …or if you're found whistling.

HENRY: (*as parent*) …or if you're five minutes late.

EDWARD: (*as child*) Can't we just go to school?

CATHERINE: You can if your parents pay. But the punishment for making a mistake is probably being caned over the hand!

EDWARD: (*as child*) What was the queen doing about it?

JAMES: The queen married Prince Albert. When he died she cut herself off from her people for years. She probably didn't know or care how much they were suffering.

EDWARD: It's horrible!

WILL: (*sings*) *Ho-rib-bull Hiss-tor-ree, why we have to learn it's a miss-tor-ree! Here's the scene, Victorean.*

(*Others join in a stately dance and sing.*)

HENRY: *As a queen, Vic was mean.*

CATHERINE: *Always fat, never lean.*

JAMES: *Fell for Albert when nineteen,*

MARY: *When he died, she weren't seen.*

ALL: *She weren't keen.*

EDWARD: *Dreadful wars – like Crimean;*

ELIZABETH: *Awful slums – water green;*

JAMES: *For the poor, not a bean:*

WILL: *That's the scene*

ALL: *Victorean.*

(*They are interrupted by* MINDE's *voice. Lights change back to classroom.*)

MINDE: My plane has landed. I am on my way

to the school by taxi at this very
moment. I will be with you in ten
minutes. I hope you are ready. If not
then you will suffer.

SCENE THIRTEEN

JAMES: Well. Henry?

HENRY: What are you looking at me for?

EDWARD: You said you were in charge.

HENRY: Look, you worm, I can't do the
impossible.

ELIZABETH: We have to know something about the
First World War.

JAMES: It was fought from 1914 till 1918. The
British Empire and the French and the
Americans were fighting against the
Germans. And...

HENRY: Good! I like history when it's about
fighting.

EDWARD: It wasn't all about fighting.

HENRY: What do you know?

EDWARD: My great grandfather told me a story
before he died.

HENRY: About war and violence and hatred?

EDWARD: In a way.

MARY: So tell us, Edward.

(*Lights change. The stage blocks become parapets and the students soldiers.* HENRY *and* CATHERINE *on the German side.* EDWARD *narrates and takes part in the action while the others mime some of the action.*)

EDWARD: (*as Eddie, narrative voice*) They called me Eddie. I'd been in the army just a few months when the war started. December 1914 was the first Christmas I'd ever spent away from home. I was a bit miserable, but the lads were good. Especially my mate Jimmy. I said to him, Jim!

JAMES: (*as Jimmy*) Aye?

EDWARD: (*as Eddie*) It's quiet, isn't it?

JAMES: (*as Jimmy*) It's Christmas. It's like an unofficial truce. We won't bother Jerry and he won't bother us. So you just enjoy your Christmas.

EDWARD: (*as Eddie*) I've got me chocolate and me tobacco and me Christmas card from the King and Queen! It's in His Majesty's own handwriting too. It says, "May God protect you and bring you home safe." (*Narrative voice*) And I was just going to say how quiet it was when I heard this sound! (*Brass band*

plays "Silent Night") The Germans
were playing Christmas carols!

HENRY: (*as Heinrich, sings*) *Stille nacht, Heilige
Nacht...*

EDWARD: (*as Eddie, jumps up*) Happy Christmas,
Fritz!

JAMES: (*as Jimmy, drags him down*) Get your
head down, Eddie, or get it blown off!

HENRY: (*as Heinrich*) Happy Christmas,
Tommy!

EDWARD: (*as Eddie*) See! They're friendly!

HENRY: (*as Heinrich*) Come here, Tommy.
Shake hands. You don't shoot. We
don't shoot.

EDWARD: (*as Eddie, narrative voice*) Jimmy tried
to stop me but a lot of the lads left the
trenches and met the Germans in No-
man's land. Someone produced a
football. I were good at football. Then
someone suggested a game and I got
picked as right winger. (*They have a
slow-motion game of football with no
ball while* EDWARD *narrates and
sometimes takes part*) For an hour there
were no war – but there were plenty of
conflict! Every time I ran forward I
were tripped by this big German.
(*Enacts a series of trips, hacks and body
checks that leave him limping while*

84

crowd react) There were just five minutes to go and we were one–nil down. I got the ball and ran to their goal. I saw the big German charging towards me! He skidded over the frozen mud in a slide that would have broken my ankle. I jumped over his legs and ran on. The goalkeeper dived too soon. I waited and slid the ball between the goalposts!

JAMES: (*as Jimmy*) Well done, Eddie lad!

EDWARD: (*as Eddie, narrative voice*) Then the whistle went for full time and I were mobbed by my team. When I turned round the German were standing there.

HENRY: (*as Heinrich*) Shake hand, Englishman. Good played.

EDWARD: (*as Eddie, shy*) Good played, Fritz.

HENRY: (*as Heinrich*) Not Fritz. Heinrich.

EDWARD: (*as Eddie*) My name Edward. Good played Heinrich.

HENRY: (*as Heinrich*) Good played Edward. Good shoot.

EDWARD: (*as Eddie*) Thanks.

HENRY: (*as Heinrich*) Today shoot football. Tomorrow shoot guns.

EDWARD: (*as Eddie*) Aye. (HENRY *turns away to return to his trench*) Heinrich! (HENRY

stops and turns) Good luck. May God
protect you and bring you home safe.

(HENRY *puts out a hand. They shake and
hold it for a while. The lights change
back to the classroom.* HENRY *holds the
handshake.*)

SCENE FOURTEEN

HENRY: Having to kill someone you like.
That's the most horrible history of all.

EDWARD: Yes.

HENRY: Look, mate, you're not very good at
History, are you. I mean … you must
be worried about this test.

EDWARD: A bit.

HENRY: (*turns to others who are looking on with
interest*) You all elected me your leader.
So I haven't just got power. I've got to
look after you.

ELIZABETH: Responsibility.

HENRY: That's the word.

CATHERINE: But what can you do?

EDWARD: He'll come up with a plan to defeat
Master Minde and his horrible history
test.

MARY: Good old Henry! What's the plan?

HENRY: Ah, well … well…

EDWARD: It's obvious!

HENRY: Even Edward can see it!

JAMES: So what is it?

HENRY: You tell them, Edward.

EDWARD: We just barricade the door to stop him getting in!

ALL: Great idea, Henry. Well done Henry!

WILL: Be quick! He's due right now!

(*They set about it, moving stage blocks to door and crouching behind them. There is a silence, all eyes on the door. Slowly the cupboard door behind them opens and a figure steps out, unseen by the characters but in full view of the audience.* MINDE *has a teacher's gown but with a full hood that hides a face covered in a grotesque rubber mask. He sits in the throne-chair and waits.* CATHERINE *turns and sees him.*)

CATHERINE: (*to* MINDE) We're going to show that Master Swine where to get off.
            (*Double take – screams. The others see* MINDE *and scatter.* EDWARD *moves upstage so he is behind the chair. The voice of* MINDE *is amplified.*)

MINDE: Now you will see just how horrible

87

history can be. You will face the terror of the test!

EDWARD: (*jumps forward and clamps the* MINDE's *arm to the chair*) Maybe we should test the teacher! (*To audience*) What do you think?

HENRY: Well done Ed.

MINDE: (*reaches across, grabs* EDWARD's *arm and clamps it into the second clamp on the chair arm*) Hah! It seems that your little friend is facing the same test! He will suffer as much as I do from the wrong answers.

EDWARD: I'll fail!

HENRY: Don't worry. We'll help you. James knows more than an encyclopaedia! And those kids in the corridor might be able to help. (*To audience*) Would you?

MINDE: They don't know as much as *I* do! (*Mechanically*) The Battle of Hastings was fought in 1066. Columbus discovered America in 1492. The Great Fire of London was in 1666…

MARY: Oh, shut up!

CATHERINE: Yeah! Shut up.

MARY: History isn't about dates and facts. It's about people. People like us.

CATHERINE: Yeah! People like me. I was executed by Henry VIII, you know.

MINDE: So ask your questions and do your worst. You'll lose and your little friend will die!

JAMES: Question one ... Henry the Sixth had eight wives. True of false?

MINDE: True!

(*A blinding flash of blue light strikes him and he twitches and cries.*)

JAMES: Wrong! It was Henry the Eighth who had six wives.

MINDE: My question! What were the symptoms of the Black Death?

ELIZABETH: (*reprises song with help of audience*)
First you feel a little poorly, then you start to swell...
Swelling, smelling and spitting blood.

EDWARD: Swelling, smelling and spitting blood.

(*They wait for blue zap but it doesn't come.*)

HENRY: Queen Victoria was the longest reigning monarch in Britain. True of false?

MINDE: True!

HENRY: False! She was one of the shortest! In fact she was tiny! Hah!

MINDE: (*zapped*) That's not fair! My question!

	Name two kings who were the only ones of that name?
WILL:	Good King Wenceslas!
MINDE:	*Engish* kings!
WILL:	Stephen!
MINDE:	Correct! One more.
WILL:	(*With audience help*) John!

(*They wait for blue light.* EDWARD *is safe.*)

CATHERINE:	Now it's your turn. Where is Hadrian's Wall?
MINDE:	From the Tyne to the Solway!
CATHERINE:	Wrong! It's at the bottom of Hadrian's garden!
MIND:	That's cheating. History isn't a joke! It's serious!
CATHERINE:	Wrong!

(MINDE *is zapped. He falls lifeless in the chair.*)

EDWARD:	I think we've killed him!

(JAMES *releases him.*)

HENRY:	He's an old guy. Probably had a weak heart. It wasn't our fault.

ELIZABETH: Maybe we should give him the kiss of life.

WILL: (*pulling back hood*) Yeuch! You can do it, Catherine. It'll be just like kissing a mirror for you.

CATHERINE: No. It'll be like kissing a rubber mask. That's all it is!

HENRY: So who's underneath it? Take the mask off him, Ed.

EDWARD: Me?

HENRY: Yeah.

(EDWARD *pulls off mask to reveal* MISS GAME.)

JAMES: Master Minde is Miss Game. Minde is Game … Mind-game. That's all it was.

MISS GAME: (*groans and stirs*) You win, then.

MARY: Why did you play that trick on us?

MISS GAME: Seemed like a good way to teach you some history.

JAMES: I thought you were a Drama teacher.

MISS GAME: Same thing really. Learning about how people behave. In the past or in this classroom today. Learning about yourselves.

HENRY: Drama's fun but History's boring!

EDWARD: I've had fun.

(*General murmur of agreement.*)

WILL: So History's fun when it's horrible, is that right?

(WILL *starts the song. Each takes a verse and they good-naturedly mock one another's attempts at rhyming.*)

WILL: *Ho-rib-bull Hiss-tor-ree, why we have to learn it's a miss-tor-ree!*

HENRY: *I'm Henry the Eighth, so don't mess with me mate-th*
I love lots of food and I eat off big plate-th

MARY: *I'm Mary the First, how the Protestants cursed*
When my fires made them sizzle and frizzle and burst!

CATHERINE: *And I am queen Cath, and she didn't half laugh*
When her Dad lopped my head and it rolled down the path!

JAMES: *And I am King Jim, I'm much better than him*
Yet all of my people insist I'm quite dim!

WILL: *I'm William the Third, and it seems quite absurd*
That I fell from my horse ... and it

didn't half hurd!

ELIZABETH: *I am good queen Bess, and I think you can guess,*
I am the best queen ever ... well, more or less!

EDWARD: (*struggles but gets there in the end ... sort of*)
Now old Master Minde, could be really unkind
But Horrible History will always get the better of him ... he'll find.

ALL: *Ho–rib–bull Hiss–tor–ree, why we have to learn it's a miss–tor–ree!*

(*School bell rings and cast begin to collect their belongings and leave.*)

MISS GAME: So what have you learned?

JAMES: I think they've learned that history's not so boring after all.

MARY: Because it's not about dead people – it's about real people. (*Meaningfully to* JAMES) Pompous people ... like you.

JAMES: (*retaliates*) Argumentative people like you!

(*They turn and start to leave, still arguing.*)

MARY: I'm *not* argumentative!

JAMES: You're arguing now!

93

MARY: I am *not* arguing…

JAMES: (*laughing*) You are! If you were my queen I'd put poison in your tea.

MARY: If I were *your* queen I'd drink it!

(*They exit laughing, arm in arm.*)

ELIZABETH: (*to* MISS GAME) History's full of people just like those kids outside in the corridor. All sorts of people. It would be dead boring if we were all the same. History's full of people like me – natural leaders!

CATHERINE: And me! Natural followers. (*Follows* ELIZABETH) I think you'd make a great queen, Elizabeth!

ELIZABETH: (*sighs*) I can't argue with that.

(*They exit.*)

EDWARD: There are a lot of victims.

HENRY: (*wraps an arm around his shoulder*) That's 'cos there are a lot of bullies around. You have to watch out for them, Ed. Come on, mate, let's go home.

(*They exit.*)

94

MISS GAME: (*to* WILL, *who is last in the room*) And what have you learned?

WILL: That there are a few laughs in History if you know where to look! There are even laughs in learning dates!

MISS GAME: (*surprised*) Are there?

WILL: Yeah! I mean, can you tell me ... on what date did Christopher Columbus sail to America?

MISS GAME: I don't know. On what date did Christopher Columbus sail to America?

WILL: He didn't sail on a date – he sailed on a ship!

(*He laughs and exits while* MISS GAME *winces.*)

MISS GAME: Time to go home, Will. (*Quietly to audience*) Time to go home.

CURTAIN